Social Media

Marketing Strategies for Twitter, Facebook, Snap Chat, LinkedIn and Instagram

Jonathan Martin

Jonathan Martin

Jonathan Martin

Table of Contents

Introduction

The arrival of social media has changed the means by which we interact with each other. It has revolutionized communication systems and created a new structure of society. Media and marketing, while having been a little slow on the uptake, are slowly realizing the vast potential and power of social media. Research indicates that the rapidly growing audience of social media spends more than 22% of their lives on these sites. Further, social media breaks boundaries of caste, religion, nation, and gender to provide a brand an outreach into all kinds of demographics.

The distinctive features of social media are: virality, and user generated content. Virality refers to the potential of content posted by a user to be shared by other users. Twitter's retweet button provides a convenient method to do this. The successful social network thus has a simple formula; some users create content, and then this content is circulated around to their large user-base, to become viral. Virality lasts for anything between a few minutes to several hours, but each piece of content is eventually replaced by other pieces of content. The next revolution in this regard has been the entry of social networks into smartphones. With it now being possible to reach a significantly larger number of people around the world at once who may not have access to a laptop or a computer, but do have a smartphone, social networks have awakened to the importance of this audience.

How do brands incorporate social media into their marketing strategy? How do they best take advantage of interacting with this massive audience? How does this influence the voice of the brand? This is what this guide will help you with. It will provide some marketing strategies to help your brand have a social media presence that complements your brands work and shows your brand in a creative and interesting light to existing customers as well as the target group. I would like to thank you for choosing to purchase this book, and hope it helps you in your attempts to find the perfect social media strategy for your brand.

Chapter 1

Identifying The Best Social Network

Each popular social network has different characteristic selling point, different kinds of content, and most importantly, different kinds of people. Most advertisers simply create accounts on all kinds of social media, but that is a potentially damaging thing to do. Identifying the best social network requires you to ask two questions:

What kind of people do I want to reach?

Each social media platform has a different demographic. Identifying the target group of whom exactly your content is meant for can position your brand better to those who actually need it. For example, if you want to reach out to photographers, you can use Instagram and Pinterest better than, say, WordPress. Similarly, if you want to reach artists, the best social networks to use can include Tumblr as well as the aforementioned. People with business interests usually have an account in LinkedIn. In any scenario, an account in Facebook and Twitter is probably viable owing to the fact that a majority of people has an account in these sites.

What kind of content do I want to post?

Social media thrives on the principle of content generation. Every social network allows you access to a certain audience who appreciate a certain kind of content. Writers, for example, are best-suited using blogs because of the space offered to them and their statistical and research tools. Brands that want to focus on one-on-one conversations will find Twitter best suited for this kind of content. LinkedIn works best for B2B based content. Yet again, Facebook and Twitter are the functional choices in most situations owing to their massive audience.

The best social media platform for your brand is thus one that includes a large portion of your target group amongst its audience, and allows you to post the kind of content you want. Instead of simply making accounts in all kinds of social media platforms, a beginner at social media marketing should start at one social network, and depending on the reaction and user-base, then look at diversifying into more social networks. Facebook and Twitter are the safest choice in this regard because of their depth of advertising options, large and truly global audience of all shapes and sizes and support to all kinds of different content.

The voice of the brand

Figuring the voice of the brand is an important step that a social media marketing strategy requires above all. Since your brand can use social media to interact with potential and existing customers on an individual manner, your brand can have a distinctive voice. This voice can be built up over time. This voice is a distinctive tonality that can allow customers to identify your brand. Customers associate your brand with a certain identity and this helps the brand maintain uniformity in posting style and content. Red Bull is a fine example. Over time, Red Bull has associated itself with a tone of adventure and sports. Their posts on Facebook do not even mention Red Bull very much, if at all, and focus on images and videos of adventures. When the record-breaking jump from outer space commenced, Red Bull live streamed the entire event on their Facebook page. They have associated their brand with a certain voice, and once you do that, the content will keep coming.

And the content needs to keep coming. Social media is a content consuming machine, as it is content over anything else that allows these vehicles to thrive. Social media marketing needs a constant influx of content to keep letting your brand be relevant, trendy and on top of things. A social media marketing strategy needs to be aware of viral things happening in the world, and incorporate these into their marketing strategy. Social media leaves a brand with no excuse to be cognizant about the world around us.

Direct communication also helps with an oft-underrated part of social media that is actually very important – customer service. Since customers can now lodge their grievances on social media, and this complaint can go viral, a brand is obliged to respond to complaints in a timely and constructive manner. A prompt and effective response to a customer can show the brand in a positive light. Responses to customer complaints and feedback are also a way to build the voice and tone of the brand.

The voice of the brand is the tone with which it would like to be heard. Different strategies call for different voices. A technological start-up aimed at teenagers may have a better chance with a quirky, brash and suggestive tone, while this voice will not be effective for investors, who may prefer a more suave and sophisticated approach. Identifying the desired audience and speaking to them in a voice they understand and appreciate are the hallmarks of any marketing strategy – and this particularly influences social media.

Of course, nothing can succeed without good and relevant content. The target group may be swayed by the tone of the brand, but if ultimately the content is shallow, your brand is not going to be able to have any sticking power with your audience. This is also where a committed brand voice can help you. Once you know the way you want to speak with your audience, you shall be able to create great content that allows you to speak to your audience this way. Your voice shall always affect your content, and keeping a voice that best fits your goals can help your content be as good as it possibly can be.

Advertising

A large aspect of marketing in social media is advertising. Advertising works on a different basis on social media because it allows you to specifically focus on your target group. The wealth of options available with social media advertising means that even small brands can, with the right advertisement strategy increase participation and engagement with audiences manifold. Once the brand has an established audience, social media can be used to announce contests, activities and campaigns, introduce new products or make an important announcement.

A well-planned advertising strategy on social media includes the following:

Goals

You need to know what you want to do with the advertisement. Do you need more engagement on your page? Do you need to highlight a specific product? Do you want to increase the number of visits on your website? Depending on your goal, your overall marketing strategy can be shaped because of the wealth of advertising options available to you. If you're just setting up, the most worthwhile goal is to try to get more followers, and help them get engaged. After a point, you need not worry about followers, as when the brand gets popular more and more people will follow the page as it has a lot of followers, the boost in popularity triggering a domino effect.

Target Group

You need to who your advertisement is aimed for. Platforms such as Facebook and Twitter allow you to be very flexible in terms of what kind of people you want to reach. People can be targeted on the basis of all kinds of demographics for your choice. Even the strictest and most inflexible social media network will have more options in terms of targeting than any other form of marketing because of the personalized one-on-one interactions possible with social media. You can also be specific with your targets, for a lower cost, however this will reach fewer people who satisfy such a criteria. Broader ranges obviously cost more. Knowing exactly what your target group is will allow you to set the most appropriate criteria for your advertisement and save you some money.

Headline

As with all advertisement in today's climate, the headline is perhaps the most important part of advertisements on social media. More than anything else, the constant flow of content means that to make your content more memorable and more worthy of attention a catchy headline is a necessity. Social media favors content with images, giving images pride of place in their feeds as well as in their advertisements. Facebook, for example, permits only 20% of text in advertisements. Thus the headline needs to be something that relates to the image and catches the attention of the audience. Text on the advertisement other than the headline needs to be clear and direct, and preferably include a call to action to give viewers a reason to click on the ad.

Offers

Advertisements on social media platforms are often the best ways to include offers. Social networks allow advertisements to appear only to those whom they think would be interested in your product according to their algorithms. This is possible because of the personal data that audiences upload onto these sites. Thus there is a good chance that the people viewing your ad are interested in your product. Thus to add an offer, such as a promo code allowing the viewer a discount will increase engagement with your brand as a whole.

Boosted Posts

Regarded as somewhat unethical for some, a boosted post is content that, with a one-time investment rises to the top of the feeds of audiences, increasing the likelihood that more people will see it. While big companies have little need of boosted posts, a smaller company can use a boosted post to create engagement for a new product launch, a contest or an activity. This can increase overall engagement of audiences with your social media page.

Chapter 2: Content Is King

As in all marketing, the content of your engagement activities is likely to draw the best kind of attention from audiences. While you can use short-term strategies such as advertisements and offers, the content of your social media page can be a promotional tool as well as a tool that sustains and builds the connections you have established using those strategies. While getting people interested in your social network is not as difficult as it may seem, keeping them interested is the most important task of your social media marketing strategy.

The nature of virality on the internet means that your content must catch the eye, but to keep your content interesting you also need your content to be broad and have depth – it must not be a transparent attempt at some catchy lines as those, while eliciting brief attention from audiences do not secure it. Content can be of many different kinds, and you must choose the best styles of content that fit the image and voice of your brand, the audiences it wants to reach, and the brand itself. However you do have the freedom to experiment with content and find out what your specific audience likes to see.

Content can be educational, or informational. A popular form of content is promotional content, where you use contests, offers and giveaways to create larger amount of interest from your audience. Content like this can also offer you some useful content of another kind – user generated content which can be posted on your page regularly. While they seem to be secondary to the content you want to post, they can be used creatively as well. Content which converses with the audience is another way of promoting your brand and its voice. Platforms allowing for easy and targeted communication, such as Twitter, are ideal for this purpose. Twitter allows your brand to engage with other popular brands, gaining more attention. However, a stiff, formal voice rarely works on such platforms, which appropriate more attention to quirky and witty conversations.

Tips for effective content

Effective content is content that not only promotes your brand but also allows you to have meaningful conversations with your audience. This gives your brand a unique identity that audiences can relate to. In the staccato beats of today, an emotional connection is actually the most solid framework your brand can rely upon in social media. To return to an earlier example, Red

Bull has formed an emotional connection for its audience with the concept and thrill of adventure. It doesn't even need to use the name of the brand on the page for its audiences to associate the brand with such a concept. They have managed this with effective content that understands the value of the medium of social media, and with a sustained, distinctive and unique voice, which has led them to building this identity. Here are some tips for your brand to do the same:

Regularity

The nature of virality on the Internet is such that it is estimated that the average post only remains on feeds for about 15 minutes. This means that a good marketing strategy involves the need to keep posting regularly, so as to keep audiences engaged with the brand. If you don't, you will need to keep promoting your social platform every time you need it, which renders the most useful aspects of social media moot. Global brands need to post every few hours to keep its audiences in all the time zones engaged. A professional managing service such as Hoot Suite is invaluable in this context to maintain a schedule of posts and make managing the posting of content easier.

Cross-platforming

Cross platforming means the use of other social media along with the main social network in which the content is being posted. This is a delicate process that requires you to understand the characteristics of all the social networks involved as well as the differences in the audiences of the brand in each of these platforms. Posting the same content is obviously not recommended, but cross platforming can be used to help other networks add on to or better develop content on your main platform. They can be used to generate more awareness for contests and giveaways. An important facet of cross-platforming is hence to not go too overboard, too many networks and you may be over burdened, and social media with posts ranging from years ago is not good for business. Keep your brand to the most popular and the most suited networks, and focus your attention on them. Keep separate plans for each of them, suited to their unique characteristics and how they allow you to be flexible in terms of what your goal from each is. For example, you can use Twitter for engagement, Facebook as your main communication portal and another service, such as Instagram or Snapchat to promote your brand. Your individual strategies for each portal would thus differ.

Value

While the occasional joke and witticism is welcome, the majority of your feed should not be dominated by them, unless if they creatively fit your brand voice. Ask yourself before posting what value these posts adds to the audience. Using social media simply to promote your brand is a reductive approach – respect its potential to actually engage your customers. Content with real value is also most likely to be shared by your audience, a major promotional tool for any brand.

Voice

As mentioned before, a unique style and tonality should be maintained for your content. While this is not necessary in any means, the nature of the internet where posts remain on feeds for just fifteen minutes or less means that a distinctive style can help make your content striking and interesting for audiences. This helps in building a brand image that transcends the social network.

Interactions

Social media platforms allow you to interact directly with your audience. Try to keep them engaged by asking them to contribute opinions, and even content. For example, a soft drink brand can ask its audiences how they use the brand to form their own drinks, and then share these recipes. Interaction allows you to understand your audience and better utilize your connections with them to come up with more well directed and well received content. You can also use the social media platforms as a public relation method for reaching out to a large audience and getting your side of the story across. Increasing news channels use social media for their news.

Awareness

Stay aware of whatever is happening around you. News tends to spread very quickly in this age of information, and therefore you must always assume your audience knows all that is happening around you. Posts can be made inappropriate because of an event happening elsewhere. During a natural disaster or tragedy, cancel your scheduled posts and treat the occasion with respect. A bad reaction in this context is a blemish on your brand, which may not be very simple to resolve. On the other hand, during a festive season you may add some content reflecting the festival.

Netiquette

Netiquette refers to the common set of rules based on etiquette on the web. These are rules that apply to all platforms, but are particularly true for the Internet where mistakes can be pounced upon by the entire world. Avoid spelling and grammar mistakes, as that indicates a lax attitude towards the interactions. If you make a mistake nevertheless, edit it immediately and apologize for the error. Fact check each piece of information you post and be ready to back whatever you say. Do not spam your audience with sustained posting of little value. Do not use hashtags indiscriminately as that is a major turn-off to audiences.

Honesty

In its essence, social media allows a brand to interact with audiences as if it a single person. This single 'person' becomes the identity of the brand. An honest and sincere attitude works much better compared to a closed off approach as audiences become more savvy with the information available to them. Social media allows you to present your brand as real, and human. This comes with the necessary ethical considerations. Core values that are respected in a human will be respected in a brand as well, such as transparency, willingness to listen to criticism, and a sincere attitude. These will allow your brand to recover from mistakes but more importantly be trusted by its customers. Maintain your ethical guidelines and stick to these while posting content.

Jonathan Martin

Chapter 3

Listening to Customers: Data

One of the most important aspects of using social media for marketing purposes is the wealth of data available to be analyzed. These can help you understand how your brand identity is being perceived, how specific kinds of content were received and what the audience demographic is like. Platforms such as Facebook, Twitter and LinkedIn have their own data algorithms, but third party software is also available which can allow you to fine-tune your analyses to your specific needs.

Data can be of two kinds: Quantitative and Qualitative. This distinction is made on the basis of how the data is used.

Quantitative Data

Quantitative data is by far the simpler data to analyze and understand. It measures numerical parameters collected via social media, which is then subject to statistical analysis. They can help you understand the specific areas your social marketing strategy needs to address. These include data like number of followers, reach, which is the level of engagement throughout the platform. Reach allows you to measure the individual impact of a single post. Since reach measures engagement levels rather than just the numbers, it is a more useful tool than the number of followers.

Click-through rate refers to the amount of clicks generated on any links posted on social media. Similar to reach, it measures the levels of engagement your audience has with your posts.

Time is interestingly one of the most important data that can be collected. By time, we mean the specific time when audiences are engaged with your page. You can measure what the best time to make a post is relative to your unique audience. Given that a post is on newsfeeds for a very short amount of time, posting your most important announcements and content at these times can maximize audience engagement with your content. While looking at the comments and engagement on a post can give you an idea of this time, more sophisticated tools are provided with third-party software.

Qualitative Data

Qualitative data is, by definition, less accurate and specific and difficult to analyze. They refer to the quality of engagement rather than the numbers. They include Trending topics, which drive conversations. These are the topics that a majority of the audience is talking about. Perception and Influence are other such data metrics, but suffer from the lack of a uniform and well-accepted way to measure such data. Both measure how its audience sees your brand and how its content is perceived. If you wish to use such data metrics, be cautious and revise all the different methodologies available to you.

Using Data Effectively

Data is of no use if it is not used effectively. To begin with, data should not be collected for the sake of collecting data. Instead, it should be collected with a specific goal in mind. Data collected with a specific perspective can take on a different meaning and be more helpful for you to analyze than just raw data without an end goal in mind. Data that is of no use to the brand is referred to with the term of insight paralysis. Data can indicate what kind of content your audience likes and dislikes, and therefore it is important to actually listen to the data, and engage audiences with what they seem to prefer. There is no hard and fast rule to set about doing this, but social media allows you the luxury to experiment and figure out the best voice, and best kind of content that you must post. The most important and commonly used way of using data is to pitch new strategies for use in the future.

Chapter 4

Marketing Strategies for Twitter

Twitter is one of the most popular social networking sites that provide a platform for users to post short messages called 'tweets' for everyone in their network to see. Statistics show that nearly 100 million users login to Twitter daily. With its user base multiplying on a regular basis, Twitter stands as one of the most popular social networking sites to market a brand or a product.

Most novices of social media marketing make the mistake of underutilizing Twitter. All they mostly do is slap up links of their products or services in their tweets. If that's the only way you use Twitter to market your product, don't expect to amass followers or make big sales.

Twitter is one social networking platform that has the power to make unknown names or brands popular in a fortnight. Unfortunately, most businessmen and marketers fail to see its true potential. The problem is that, they see twitter as only a platform that allows posting of short messages and fail to think beyond the tweets. To get a grasp of how powerful Twitter is, and to utilize it to its full potential, you need to first understand how Twitter actually works and also why it works the way it does.

Let us first see what makes twitter a successful social media platform:

1. Forming a network is easy on Twitter as it is a personal-choice based platform. Unlike solicitation-based social networking sites like Facebook, which involves sending invitations or friend requests to become a part of a network, Twitter doesn't involve any form of solicitation. You don't need to send requests to follow someone's tweets, and you don't have to accept requests to let someone else follow your tweets.

2. It allows you to post short, quick messages in real-time. When compared to Facebook, which requires a user to follow several steps to post something, messages can be posted pretty quickly on Twitter.

3. The number of characters in a tweet is limited to 140, and so the users can't post lengthy (and boring) messages.

This kind of format suits the 'no time to breathe' attitude of the present generation.

4. Communication is the main motto of Twitter. It is an ideal tool for communicating something to large number of people quickly and easily.

You need to focus and make optimal use of the above-mentioned factors in order to make your presence felt and successfully market your product on Twitter. Most importantly, you need to focus on #4 to make it big on Twitter.

First and foremost, you need to have a basic understanding of how Twitter can be used as a marketing tool.

As a marketing tool, Twitter can be used to:

- Promote your brand

- Build client base for your product or service

- Achieve focused networking, that doesn't involve sending awkward requests

- Redirect people to your websites or blogs

But not all people manage to effectively use Twitter in promoting their products. Basically, your success on Twitter depends on how you approach the platform, and how well you make use of its features.

Let's see how you need to approach Twitter, before learning how to make efficient use of its various features.

As mentioned earlier, Twitter is easier to use when compared to other social networking sites. If Twitter is so ideal and easy-to-use, why doesn't every Twitter marketing strategy become a success? Let's approach this question with an example. Let's suppose you are a freelance photographer who posts your work on Twitter. Your work may attract attention and people might start following you. They will also start posting comments on your work, to which you'd be happy to respond. But, not everyone would want to contact you through comments. Some people who are interested in your work or service might want to contact you more personally, for example, via an email. And before doing so, they *will* take a look at your profile to know who you are. If you don't have *your* photograph as your profile picture, or if you hadn't put much thought into your bio or simply left it empty, the prospective client might think twice to contact you personally, as you offer no personal connection. He needs to see your face and read something about you before contacting you for your service.

He might also want to visit your website, but if you hadn't provided proper links to your site or had provided dead links, it won't be long before the client loses interest altogether. And Bam! You have lost a prospective client for not being informative about yourself. So, keep in mind these two golden rules while creating your account on Twitter:

Setting up an effective profile picture

Never use the default profile picture Twitter provides you (the silly egg avatar). If you continue using the same old egg as your profile picture, it gives an impression to people that you are lazy or aren't very creative, and shows your laxness towards your online presence. Also, people might think you aren't that tech-savvy, which is inexcusable nowadays. It doesn't matter how interesting your tweets are or how first class your product is, if you don't remove the silly white egg from your profile, there is no way people would take you or your product seriously. Also, people might mistake your account for a Twitter bot (a software application that automatically makes posts or follows users) and block it altogether.

It's well and good if you use your business logo as your profile picture. But if you are planning to upload your headshot (for your personal account as an entrepreneur), there are certain points you need to keep in mind. It is advised that you upload a professional headshot, if you want people to take you seriously. There's a huge difference between uploading a silly selfie and uploading a professional headshot. It is the image you portray through your photograph that will decide on how seriously people will take you. Also, it is understandable if you want your profile picture to reflect your personality, but what impression would it give a prospective client if you post a picture of yourself donning a hat that has little hearts and cupids all over it? (It's not like the hat is essential for attracting customers, so you can do away with it.)

Thus, it is important to remember that a profile picture is *important*. And it has to be *your* picture and not the picture of your car or your dog or the unimpressive egg.

Writing the best bio

Your bio is the first thing people will look at before opting to follow you. In all probability, people will base their decision to follow or not follow you based on the short bio you write in your profile. So, you need to write a few words about yourself so as to provide a quick glance of you who really are and what you do. The character count of the bio is limited to 160 characters. So, you don't get a lot of room to tell the world about yourself. It can be quite difficult to type down an impressive, eye-catching bio in such a few characters, and that is where you need to bring in your creativity and make that 'elevator speech', without going beyond the character limit.

The bio doesn't have to be written in the form of a boring paragraph

Instead of writing down what you do in a paragraph, you can put down your bio in the form of a list. That way, your bio won't look boring and people will get a clear idea of what you do, and also, you can save up on characters

For example, consider the following bio of a pet store owner written in the form of a paragraph:

A pet blogger, who is also the owner of a pet store named 'Paws and Drools' that sells puppies, kittens and offers premium foods and accessories for your pets.

The bio is pretty straightforward and is about 160 characters in length. All you can decipher form the bio is that the tweeter is a pet blogger who also owns a pet store that sells food and accessories for cats and dogs. The only information that the owner could fit in the bio is what he does for a living and the name of his store and the services it offers. There is *no personality*. Also, the owner might also be a pet expert and a pet food critic, but there is just no room to type anything further.

The bio seen above does sound professional, but it also sounds a tad boring as very little personality is reflected in the words. Also, see that your bio has a bit of a personality; you may be an entrepreneur who wants to sound professional while telling about yourself, but such bios will most probably go over people's heads.

Now, let's see how the bio can be written in the form of a list, so as to create room for a bit of a personality and extra information:

Pet blogger ▪ *Pet expert* ▪ *Pet food critic* ▪ *Pet store owner @PawsandDrools, Against animal cruelty* ▪ *Loves nature, dogs, cats, and people!*

Just look at how adding a bit of a personality changes the tone of the bio. The bio covers everything on the professional front and also lets the followers get a gist of the person's personality. And remember, a personal connection with your followers is very important. And you can establish such personal connection by going a bit personal in your bio.

In the above example, it is quite evident that the Twitter account is of the pet storeowner and not the actual pet store. The owner might have another twitter account solely dedicated to the pet store, and not about himself. In such cases, using the @ symbol leads users into the other twitter account. In the above example, the pet store owner uses the @ symbol to link to the PawsandDrools the twitter account of his pet store.

Your bio should be written by keeping your target audience in mind

The point of social networking sites is to let people who share common interests interact with each other. If your business belongs to a particular niche, the target audience would also come from the same niche. Don't be afraid to share your interests, ideologies and passions, for such information does impart a personality to your bio. Don't be afraid to mention who you are and what you believe in for the fear of offending people. There is a very less chance of those people being interested in your services anyway. There are many people on the internet who are just like you and believe in the things you do.

For example, when you create a Twitter account for your pet store, the followers it gains will obviously be pet lovers or people who are interested in buying pets Would a person who's allergic to cats or who hates pets be interested in your pet store? No. Most of the followers would be animal lovers in general and maybe concerned about the living conditions of the animals in your store.

The bio says that the pet storeowner is against animal cruelty. This gives an impression that the person is kind and treats his animals well. Also, it gives an impression that the animals at his store live in hygienic conditions. After all, first impression tends to stick in the minds of people, so it is important that you create a good first impression through your bio.

Share your Hashtags in the bio

The modified bio seems fine, but it does not show any hash tags. In general, a hash tag (#) is used by people in their tweets to denote a keyword or a phrase related to a product, event or cause. These hashtagged keywords or phrases categorize the tweets in which they are used, such that those tweets appear in the search results when someone searches for a particular topic.

Share your hashtags in your bio, if you have any. When a user clicks on a hashtag, all the tweets in which the hashtagged keyword has been used will be displayed. Thus, it is better you create a hashtagged keyword or phrase for your own business. All though most people have a love/hate relationship with the usage of hashtags (as they seem confusing), they do play an important role in promoting your product, when used in the right way (you will see how to create hashtags and how powerful they can be as a marketing tool in the next section). Here's an example of how you can use your hashtag in your bio.

Pet blogger ▪ Pet expert ▪ Pet food critic ▪ Pet storeowner @PawsandDrools, #CutePetSales▪ Against animal cruelty ▪ Loves dogs, cats, and people!

In the above bio, #P&Dpuppysale is a hashtag custom to the business, and when people click on it, all the tweets consisting of the hashtag will appear on their screen. For example, one of the customers who has recently bought a puppy from the Paws and Drools pet store might have tweeted something like-

Just bought a cute little puppy at #CutePetSales! The little fella looks so adorable and my daughter loves him to death already!

Such tweets will appear on the screen as soon as someone clicks on the #CutePetSales tag in the bio. Observe how mentioning a hashtag in your bio serves as a promotion tool for your product.

Link your websites or blogs in the bio

Remember that you can't write paragraphs about your product or interests on Twitter. Blogs or websites are the ideal places where you can do that. So, if you have a website or a blog (which is recommended), provide links to them in your bio. When people read a few lines about you or your product, they might want to know more but that doesn't mean they are going to Google your product separately. So, placing links imminent importance to redirect people to your website or blog. Placing a link to your website will look something like this:

Pet blogger ▪ Pet food critic ▪ Pet storeowner @PawsandDrools, #CutePetSales▪ Against animal cruelty ▪ Owns www.paswsndrools.com ▪ Loves dogs, cats and people!

Humor is always welcome as long as it doesn't go overboard

Using a bit of a humor imparts a playful tone to your bio. Just because you are professional doesn't mean your bio has to sound boring. But remember, the humor needs to be of good taste. If you don't think a humorous tone would be appropriate for your business, you can give it a pass.

Here's the witty Twitter bio of Hollywood actor Tom Hanks:

I am the actor in some of the movies you like and some you didn't. Sometimes I'm in pretty good shape, other times I'm not. Hey, you gotta live, you know?

Los Angeles- playtone.com

Looks witty and impressive, doesn't it? He establishes a personal connection with his followers without going overboard.

Talk about your accomplishments

People tend to weigh your business or services based on your accomplishments. So, don't feel bad about bringing up your achievements in your bio! Be proud of what you have achieved and let people know the same. It is important that people know what you have accomplished. Let's modify the bio of the pet storeowner to include one of his achievements. It may look like this:

Pet blogger • Pet store owner @PawsandDrools voted as the Best Pet Store 2014 @petsmagazine • Against animal cruelty • Loves dogs, cats and people!

www.paswsndrools.com

When people come to know that your pet store has been voted the best pet store for the year 2014, they wouldn't think 'Whoa! He is so full of himself!' They are most likely to think 'Hmm. That's impressive'. So, you don't have to be so modest when it comes to sharing your accomplishments in your bio. *It is important for your business.*

Thus, you have seen the two golden rules you need to follow while creating a profile on Twitter. Now let's move on to how well you can use its features to promote your brand.

Master the art of using Hashtags

You can't possibly imagine Twitter without those funny looking hashtags. Love them or hate them, you just can't ignore them. They may seem annoying or confusing, but when used in the right way, they can play an instrumental role in amassing followers for your account.

As we have already seen, hashtags are keywords or key phrases which are preceded by a # symbol. They aid Twitter users in searching for tweets of their interest. For example, if you type #Titanic in the search box, you get tweets about the movie and not tweets like 'who built the Titanic', as 'Titanic' is not proceeded by a hashtag in tweets like that.

How do I create a hashtag?

You can create a hashtag by simply adding a hash symbol (#) in front of a keyword or a phrase related to your business. But, before doing so, don't forget to search on Twitter if the hashtag has been taken. Hashtags are not case sensitive, which means #TITANIC and #titanic are one and the same. Also, no spaces are allowed in between the characters.

How do I make my hashtag reach people?

You can simply do so by announcing your hashtag to your followers first, by tweeting something like:

Hey guys, I have created a new hashtag for 'Paws and Drools'. Got questions, suggestions or feedback for me? Simply add #PawsandDrools to your tweet.

This way, you are announcing to your followers that this hashtags exists, which they could use while tweeting about your pet store.

But, before going ahead and creating a hashtag for your brand and using it in your tweets, keep the following points in mind:

1.   The hashtag for your product doesn't have to hold the name of the brand. You can use other interesting keywords or phrases that represent your product. For example, instead of creating the hashtag *#PawsandDrools* for your pet store, you can create a simple hashtag like *#CuteHappyPets*, while posting pictures of pets at your store. Also, your hashtags need to target a specific set of audience, and they should be able to relate to the phrase or keyword. Creating a hashtag *#PetLoversLA* (if your pet store is located in Los Angeles) is always advantageous over simply using the brand's name.

2.   *#Do #Not #Overload #your #tweets #with #hashtags.* See how annoying that looks? Using hashtags is extremely

important for marketing your product, but don't fill-up your tweet with hashtags. See that you don't use more than two hashtags in a single tweet.

3. Don't use too many characters while creating a hashtag. People may relate to hashtags like *#WeLovePetsAndTheyLoveUsBack,* but they most definitely won't use it, as it's just too long and no one would have time to remember and type out the whole phrase. Limit the number of characters in a hashtag to 20 at most.

Create your Twitter marketing Strategy

So far, we have learnt how to set up an effective Twitter profile and how to use hash tags properly. And now comes the hard part, creating a marketing strategy for your product. Don't worry; you can create a successful Twitter marketing strategy by following some simple steps.

1.   Observe and Learn from your competitors

Don't be in a hurry to create a marketing strategy; you need to do your homework first. Observe how other products belonging to the same niche as yours are being marketed. Make note of what you like about their strategy and what you do not. Now, chalk out a strategy that covers the points you've liked and excludes the points you've disliked. Also, observe how your competitors interact with their followers. Are they doing a good job? Can you improve upon the tactics they are following? Observing and learning are the keys.

2. Stick to the 80/20 principle

You might not have heard of the 80/20 principle, so here's what it says- 'Use 80% of your tweets to interact with your followers in the form of replies, favoriting and retweets. Once you make a personal connection with your followers, you can put down links, promotions or attractive offers that lead them to your website and make purchases'.

3. Don't sound too formal

People will only approach you if you seem like a friendly, approachable person. If you come across as being overly formal and boring, without letting out even a bit of your personality, people may not feel like approaching you. Use friendly, hear-warming language and come up with pleasant and authentic replies. A bit of humor and wit helps too. Your formal strategy shouldn't stop you from communicating pleasantly and friendlily with your followers.

4. Lists matter

A Twitter list is an important tool that lets you filter information. Creating a list involves grouping together of people who belong to the same niche. For instance, if you are a medical representative, you might want to create a list of all the doctors in your city, so as to interact with them more easily and keep a track of their tweets.

You can create a list by simply clicking on the settings icon (gear icon) and clicking on the 'Lists' option. In the Lists page, click on the 'create list' button and from then Twitter pretty much guides you through the process of creating a list. You can set your list to be either public or private. Sharing of your lists with other users is also possible; all you need to do is open your list, copy its URL and paste it in a tweet or a direct message.

The best way to let other users know that you've added them in a list is to notify them of the same. This is an effective way to build up your community. The notifying message might look something this:

Hi @Maurice's_petfoodsupplies, we are glad to inform you that we have added you to our #PawsAndDrools pet food suppliers list on Twitter.

5.   Include Images and Videos of your work environment

A study conducted by Twitter revealed that posting an image in a tweet results in the boosting of retweets by 35%. Posting a video has shown to have boosted retweets by up to 28%. So it is advised that you include images or videos of your business operations and what you do behind the scenes. For example, you could post a friendly photograph of you petting one of the pups or kittens of your pet store. You can also include behind the scene images of how you feed and clean the pets.

Or if you own a bakery, besides posting gorgeous images of the cakes you sell, you can also include behind the scene images of how your bakers make the cakes. If you own a restaurant, you can post videos of how your chef meticulously flips the pan. The video or image must give a gist of the work environment of your business to your followers. If you are an artist, post images of you working on a canvas.

6. Attract followers with helpful tips

People love useful tips. Providing tips related to your niche is an easy way to attract followers. If you are a pet storeowner, you can provide tips on how to groom a dog or on how to control fleas and ticks on a pet. If you are a chef, put down tips related to cooking or tweet simple recipes. People need to know that you are knowledgeable of your niche and should also find your tips valuable.

Jonathan Martin

7. Respond to mentions and comments

Responding to a comment or a mention shows someone that you take your account seriously and are an approachable individual. Even though replying to a comment is the best way to respond to someone, it may not be possible if you have a huge number of followers. In such cases, you can acknowledge a comment or a mention by simply 'favoriting' it. Using this feature lets other people know that you have acknowledged or liked their tweet. But, don't overdo it. If you keep on endlessly favoriting the tweets or mentions made by your followers, Twitter may suspend your account, as it mistakes your over-favoriting as the work of a bot, which automatically favorites tweets.

Also, favorite only the appropriate tweets. Don't go on favoriting every tweet that mentions your brand, especially without reading them first. Look at the tweet below:

The dog food I bought at @PawsAndDrools is not of the best quality. Not visiting it again.

If you go ahead and favorite the above tweet without reading it, just because it has mentioned your business, it would be pretty awkward as people can see what you have favorited on your profile.

8. Include news or articles by industry experts

Retweet the content posted by industry experts or mention them in your tweets, so that your followers can learn more of them. Link relevant blogs or articles that would benefit your business. For example, providing links to pet blogs or articles by pet experts may encourage people to learn more of their pets and it gives them an impression that you tweet quality content.

Also, if you are in the business of bath oils, post links to research articles or news that emphasizes bath oils as being therapeutic or good for skin.

9. Make efficient use of the retweet button

You might want to share a tweet that has positively reviewed or mentioned your product. When you retweet, the original tweet will be notified of the retweet, but there is no way for him to thank you back through the notification panel. For doing so, he needs to search for the tweet in your profile, which is too much of a hassle.

So, don't just limit yourself to using the retweet button. To facilitate easy acknowledgement of your retweets, you can copy and paste the content of the original tweet into a new tweet, and prefix the text with the letters RT.

9.   Make use of Twitter analytics

A new feature named Twitter analytics can help you keep track of your tweets, retweets, clicks, favorites and other tweet engagements. But, to gain access to the feature, you need to register for Twitter ads first. But there's nothing to worry, you are not obligated to make any ad purchases, you are just expected to provide the name of your business, email-id and credit card details. Do not fret, Twitter won't charge you unless you actually purchase an ad.

Twitter Directories

So far, we have seen how one can create an efficient Twitter strategy for his/her business, but is there a way for Twitter users to find out about your business outside of Twitter? Most users on Twitter are unaware of the fact that they can register their Twitter profiles on a directory. These directories aid users greatly in marketing your product to the target audience. Here are the advantages of registering your profile on a Twitter directory:

> ➤ You can gain followers free of cost by registering in one of the twitter directories. Other users of the directory who share common interests with you can come across your profile and follow it. There is also a very less chance of these followers being spam.

➢ In these directories, you can also discover people to follow, or make business associations with. You can search for tweeps (users who tweets) based on the categories of your interest. Who knows? You might find your future business partner on these directories.

➢ Most of these directories also offer pro-services, which means that they charge a small fee to feature your Twitter profile wherever they can. Such small investments may lead to big successes.

Here are some of the popular Twitter directories on which you can register your profile:

WeFollow

While registering on WeFollow, you get to choose five of your interests, based on which your profile will be assigned to a category.

Twellow

Twellow requires you to provide your Twitter username and password while registering your profile; but don't fret, it's worth the risk. Once you register, a Twellow profile page is created for you, based on the information extracted from your Twitter profile. It suggests you the categories in which your profile has to be shown. You can either accept those suggestions or add categories of your own.

Connect.me

This site allows you to discover users and 'vouch' for other users present in your network.

Twitaholic

This directory provides a list of Twitter users based on the number of followers they have.

Twellow

Twellow is a great place to list your Twitter profile as it acts as yellow pages for Twitter.

Tweet Find

It's a free Twitter directory where you can add your Twitter account. It acts like a white and yellow page directory for Twitter users.

TwitterPacks

It is a community-based site, wherein Twitter users are recommended by their fellow users, based on their interests or location.

Twibs

Twibs is a site, which lists out hundreds of Twitter businesses. Monthly contests are held wherein people vote for businesses. This is one site where you need to list your business, as people searching for businesses often visit this site.

Listorious

Listorious is not a place where you can discover Twitter users; it's a place where you can discover Twitter lists. Listorious ranks Twitter lists based on the number of followers. You can also add a list of you own, after which your list will be given a rank too.

First Issue

If you are a budding author, you might want to register on First Issue, a directory where you can find a sea of book publishers and book traders who use twitter.

Legal Birds

If you are a lawyer or in need of one, register on Legal Birds- the site which maintains a list of lawyers, professors of law and law librarians who use twitter.

Twitter has come a long way from where it started, and keeps improving its features and tools. But, we might forget about its basics by getting caught up in the web of advance features it offers. It is important that you revisit Twitter's basic features, if you want to effectively market your product. Before chalking out a Twitter marketing strategy for your business, you need to analyze each and every one of its features, starting from the basic

Chapter 5
Marketing Strategies for Facebook

Facebook is one social networking site that has progressed rapidly from a fun site used by teenagers to an ultimate marketing hub for businesses and brands, both big and small. In recent years, a number of businesses have succeeded in attracting customer base through Facebook and there are also a number of businesses that have failed to do so. If we conduct a comprehensive study on the businesses that saw success on Facebook, we can see that the reason behind their success is an effective *strategy*.

So, you need to build an effective strategy before setting out to promote your business or brand on Facebook.

Creating an effective Facebook strategy basically involves four stages. They are:

1. Planning

2. Creating Content

4. Measuring results

Let us take a look at each of these stages in detail:

Planning

In the planning stage, you focus on and defining your target audience and defining your business' Facebook page.

1. Defining the target audience

Before you set out to create a Facebook page for your business, you need to define your target audience. You can do this by asking yourself some questions about the people your business is meant for.

1. Whom does your business target: Male customers or female customers or both?

2. What is the age group of your target audience?

3. Do they fall into a particular social class? If so, what is it?

4. How do they communicate online? Is their communication characterized by a particular tone or use of language?

5. What are they interested in?

Even if your business or brand has a broad audience, categorizing them into different groups is a great idea, as it will let you decide who is most likely to have a Facebook account and create specific content for each group.

2. Identifying the needs and problems of the customers

After defining the target audience for your business, you need to identify their needs and problems.

1. Are the target audience conscious of their looks in general?

2. Do they need to be entertained?

3. Do they stay at home always?

4. Do they need to be stimulated intellectually?

5. Do they feel lonely?

6. Are they in need of money?

You need to choose a couple or more of problems or needs that are commonly seen in your target audience. It is not that your business should be able to solve their problems, but knowing their needs and problems lets you create content that tick with them.

3. Defining your page

Now that you have a complete idea of what kind of audience you are aiming at and what kind of problems they have, you should think of what your target audience is going to get for liking your page.

Before deciding on what your page is going to offer, you need to know the top reasons why people 'like' a page. People on Facebook usually like a page for:

1. Supporting a brand they like

2. Receiving discounts or coupons

3. Receiving updates about the brand they like

4. Participating in contests

5. Sharing personal experiences they had with the brand

6. Sharing their interests with others

7. Researching brands before buying a product or service

8. Because their friends have already liked the page

9. Because of an advertisement posted online, on newspapers or magazines.

10. Because of a recommendation from a friend or a family member

It is advised that you create your content based on the needs mentioned above. If you manage to do so, you are most likely to succeed in marketing your product or brand.

Now, try writing down what your page is going to offer to your target audience in a single sentence. If you are a local business, it could be something like 'Letting the audience know of our latest products, interacting with them and staying on top of the local news.'

If you own a food business, it could be something like 'Posting pictures of food we sell and letting the audience know of the offers and discounts we offer for the weekend'

4. Deciding on an approach to reach out to audience

After defining your business page, you need to decide on how you are going to approach your target audience. You need to define your approaches to:

1. Attract and build audience for your page. This involves making the audience share your posts and interact with each other

2. Get the audience to make purchases or sign up

Let's take a look at different approaches you can employ for each of the targets mentioned above:

Approaches for attracting and building audience

There are three key approaches through which you can attract and build audience base:

a. Creating relevant and quality content

You need to focus on creating content that relevant to your business as well as appealing to the target audience. You need to be consistent with your posts and see that they are entertaining and informative at the same time. Such posts attract audience's attention and will lead to interaction among themselves in the form of comments. Also, such quality posts often get shared, which in turn aids in attracting new audience to your page. For instance, if you are running a fast food business, you can post content that has informative tone like '5 things you didn't know about cheese' or '5 benefits of eating cheese'. The posts might also be entertaining like ' 11 Pizza jokes that would make you roll on the floor laughing'. When people share your posts, word spreads about your business in their Facebook Community. People commenting or liking the post too will result in the spreading of word about your business in their communities, which attracts more and more people to do the same. Also, when you post shareable content consistently, people are more likely to visit your page often.

b. Running timeline contests

Timeline contests are an easy way to attract large number of people to like or comment on a post. Also, they result in the commentators interacting with each other, which is good for your publicity. The more people talk about your or your post, the more publicity you get. For instance, you can post a picture of a new cheese dish you have prepared and ask people to name it innovatively by commenting in the comment section. You can announce a massive discount at your food joint for the winner, which results in a large number of people sharing and commenting on your post.

c. Holding competitions/contests via apps

Besides running contests or competitions on your timeline, you can also hold contests through apps. That way, you can get more people to like your page by fang-gating the contest. It means, if a person tries to participate in your contest through an app, he will be prompted that the only way he can access the entry form is to 'like' your page. If you are running a competition, see that it is effectively publicized, as that's the only way people get to know about the contest.

c. Advertising

Targeted advertising is the best way to attract audience to your page. It is advised that a set aside a chunk of your budget (if you have one) towards advertising. The 'promote page' button or the 'boost post' button won't do much for the publicity of your page and posts. Instead, opt for either Power Editor or Ads Manager for setting up an ad. Even though you need to spend money for advertising, remember that it's totally worth your money.

Approaches to get the audience make purchases or sign up

Getting people to actually make a purchase or sign up is not very easy, but it's definitely not hard. Here are the approaches you can adopt for the purpose:

1. Again, hold competitions through an app

When people try to access a contest through an app, it gives you an opportunity to collect data like their contact number or email address.

2. Offer discounts and deals

The best way to reignite fans that have remained dormant for a long time and to attract new ones is by offering sizeable discounts or deals. For creating a real buzz, announce that the offer is time-sensitive and will expire after x hours. Don't just announce an offer out of nowhere; let the people know in advance that you are going to announce an offer. See that the offer lasts only for a small time frame.

3. Redirect people to your website

Post an attractive ad which when clicked upon will lead to your website. When the person attempts to know more information about the product or service, prompt them that the only way they can only do so by signing up for the website. For example, post an ad that says you can download a book for half the price from your website. When people click on the ad, see that it takes them to your official website. Before buying the book, they will try to read a sample of it. Then, prompt them that the only way they can read a sample from the book is by signing up for your website.

4. Offer things for free

Offering things for free doesn't mean you have to give away your products for free. You could give away things of small value like a short eBook or even a free sample of your product.

For instance, if you own a pet store, you can write a short eBook on the grooming tips for cats and dogs and offer it for free. Ask people to sign up for your website or newsletter to download the eBook for free. This approach is very beneficial in building mailing lists, which you can use to promote your pet store further.

Creating Content

So, far we have seen how you need to decide on a Facebook strategy for your business page by taking account several questions. Now, let us take a look at the different types of content you can post on Facebook, so as to grab the attention of your target audience.

Set themes for your content

Instead of posting content randomly, you can set specific themes for specific days or weeks, and post content related to the theme. Doing so helps you in focusing on your content. For instance, if you own a food joint, you can run a theme related only to pizza for a full week. You can name it something like 'Pizza is love' and post quirky snippets, jokes, observations, images or videos related to Pizza for the whole week. The following week, you can do the same for hot dogs. It is advised that you maintain a calendar for planning the themes for your content.

Using images

Using an image is always better than posting textual content alone. Images do grab the attention of the visitors, but they need to interesting, eye-catching and shareable for that to happen. You can use images for sharing different kinds of content like quotes, local news, images of customers, behind the scenes imagery etc.

Sharing quotes

Quotes are the most sharable of contents on Facebook. You can use images to make the quotes even more shareable. You can start by searching for quotes that are relevant to your business. Quotes can be added to your image using PicMonkey. Also, try to use only quotes that are of good taste; they should be pleasant, motivating or quirky. It's even better if they could generate laughs or smiles. Also, try to use quotes that haven't been shared before and try not to use quotes that were overused,

There are several sources on the internet from where you can get quotes namely, Goodreads, Brainy Quotes or even Pinterest.

Hot topics

You need to keep a track on what's currently happening in your town and use it to your advantage. Or is there a topic that's currently being widely discussed offline or online too? Can you tap into the topic by using images?

Behind the scenes Imagery

People are usually curious about what happens behind the scenes, be it a movie or a business. If you own a fast food business, you can post pictures of your chef preparing a Pizza or if you own a pet store, you can post pictures of how a puppy is being bathed by your staff.

Images of customers

One innovative way to use images is to ask your customers to post photographs of themselves enjoying your product or service on your page. Then you can award the best of them 'Fan of the week'. Also, you could post those images and ask other customers to make a caption for it.

Nostalgic Images

History interests most people, and if you could find historic or vintage photographs related to your industry or business, post them as nostalgic images. For example, you could find old black and white photographs of fast food joints, to let customers know how they looked back in those days.

Status Updates

Images do attract attention of people, but plain text statuses too have the capability to reach out to people, provided they could spark conversations. Here are the different ways you can update the statuses of your page:

Ask Questions

The best way to engage people is by asking them questions through status updates, the advantages of which are as follows:

- People tend to answer questions, and they do so through comments. More comments mean more publicity to your page.

- People who have commented and shared your status are more likely to remember your page.

- Looking at the comments will help you in finding about more about the commentators, who are none other than your audience

There are no rules when it comes to the format of the question, but the best way to do it is as follows:

Catchy headline

Ask the question you need an answer for, by including you personal experience if possible

a. First option
b. Second option
c. Third option
d. Fourth option

If you include personal experience, you will help people in picturing their own answers. When the question is given as a multiple choice question, people can simply comment the option number or letter, instead of typing the whole answer. This is especially handy for people who use Facebook on their mobile phones.

Post interesting trivia or facts

People tend to share and like interesting facts or trivia with their friends on Facebook, and also tend to remember them. If you could compile and post interesting or fun facts related to your business or industry, you could encourage people to remember and share your posts. There's always Google at your aid, if you need sources to collect interesting and unusual facts and trivia related to your industry. .

Useful tips

People love to read tips and you use this to your advantage. Also, if people find good and useful tips, they tend to share it with their friends and family on Facebook. You can share tips related to your business that you have learnt from your own experience, or you can take help of Google again to compile a list of useful tips for your audience. If you keep on posting useful tips, people will remember your page as a good source for useful tips and are sure to come back for more. That way, you can build up loyalty among your audience.

Video updates

Just like images, video posts also attract attention, especially if they are not too long. Funny, inspirational or interesting video take the cake when it comes attracting likes and comments. You can easily share tips through videos than through textual updates. Also, videos are the best media through which you can demonstrate the working of your product. One such successful video campaign is the "Will it blend' video series by BlendTec. In the videos, they demonstrate the power of their blender, but putting an iPhone into it. After people find that the blender can chew off an iPhone, it becomes obvious to them that the blender can work its magic on the lumps of a smoothie too. It is an excellent way to get noticed and make people remember your brand.

The same way, wouldn't it be great if you could make a series of videos that demonstrate the working and specialties of your product?

Post links

Never forget to post links that redirect people to your website or blog. But, don't just slap up a link on the status without any text that says what the link is about. People should know where they would go before clicking the link, and also don't just post links to the homepage of your website. See that people are redirected to a specific page, so that they don't have to search the website for the page they want.

When should you post?

Try not to post your updates between 8-9 am, which is the peak time on Facebook. When you make a post during the time, it means your content has to compete against a sea of content posted on other pages. Other than that, there are no particular rules when it comes to when you should post your content.

Measuring results

You need to measure the success of your Facebook page once in a while to see how it's going. There are several tools that help in measuring several aspects of your Facebook page. Some of the most popular ones are:

Google Analytics

Google Analytics is a very important tool that could measure how much traffic website is getting from Facebook. If haven't yet installed it on your website, do it already!

Quintly

In order to find out if people are taking notice of your brand or product, you need to know the number of people that are talking about your page (PTAT). It is difficult to find out PTAT manually, if a large number of people are interacting. So, you can use the tool Quintly to monitor PTAT of your product or brand.

Facebook insights

Facebook insight is a tool, which lets you know the demographics of your audience. It shows how many likes are from male users and how many are from female users. It also lets you know the age group and location of people who like your content.

Thus, you can make use of these tips, tricks and tools to build an effective Facebook strategy for your product.

Chapter 6
Marketing Strategies for LinkedIn

LinkedIn is a social networking site that has managed to attract the attention of businessmen and job seekers over the years. When used properly, LinkedIn can fuel the growth of your business and result in an exponential increase of your market.

There are many LinkedIn strategies you can employ to market your product or business, but it is important that you choose the one that is feasible with your budget, time and manpower.

Here are a few important and effective LinkedIn strategies you need to adopt to market your brand:

Create an impressive company page

It is very important to create your company page on LinkedIn such that it makes a good first impression on people. The company page can be thought of as an extension of your company/business website. You can make efficient use of the page by filling it up with information that directly aims at your target audience. Here are a few tips you need to follow to create an impressive company page for your brand:

- See that the page consists of expert content that answers your audience's questions and solve their problems

- Use imagery if you want the page to grab attention

- Use videos to demonstrate the workings of your product

- Use showcase pages to highlight your brand

- For encouraging click-through, see that the updates you post are short

- Try reaching more people by sponsoring the best of your content

- One way to make people advocate your brand is by revealing your company culture.

- See that your company/business website has a 'follow us' button. You can start by inviting your staff, suppliers and clientele to follow your page and over time, you will find that your page is being visited by increasing number of people every day.

Using Advanced Search tool

The best way to target your prospects through LinkedIn is by using the advanced search tool of LinkedIn.

- Go to the LinkedIn header menu, click on Search -> Advanced search.

- The advanced search lets you filter down the search down based on a number of criteria. The center column of the Advanced People Search proves to be extremely beneficial and powerful when it comes to filtering your criteria. Criteria can be filtered by:

- Currently working company

- location

- school

- University etc.

By using this tool, you can directly find your prospects. The chances of you finding the prospects suitable for your business, is directly proportional to the size of your network. Using this feature, you can search your entire network; but remember that you get the best leads only through the people connected to you on the first three levels.

Group Search

Groups can also be searched using the search feature, besides looking for prospects for your company. There are over 2 million groups that are currently active on LinkedIn. So, it is easier to find a number of groups that are associated with your industry.

Leads can be best gained by finding a relevant group, joining it and participating in the discussions. Doing so will naturally lead you to new contacts. Same features can be seen in both advanced searches and group searches, but the latter has additional features like category, language and relationship level.

Keep these features in mind while looking for groups:

Level of activity: The rank of a LinkedIn group is determined by its level of activity. So, look for groups whose level of activity is given as 'very active' in the search results.

Relevance: See that the group you find meets the criteria you have set for your target audience. See that the level of relevance is high.

Size: Don't go for the groups that are very big in number; it is difficult for your voice to be heard in such groups.

You are allowed to join up to a total of 50 groups, so joining different groups that are related to various facets of your business is advantageous over joining groups that belong to the same areas.

Create a group

Creating a LinkedIn group is essential for establishing your business or brand as an industry leader. This requires to you to search for members who have several goals in common.

For the efficient management of the group, you need to assign a responsible individual with the task of approving discussion posts, accepting members and providing moderation services for the group. The individual needs to show good judgment while accepting new members into the group.

It is not enough if you just launch a group and do nothing about it. You need to get the word out by contact your partners, clients, vendors, employees and big names of your industry if you can.

These individuals can be appointed as ambassadors for your groups and can be asked to initiate discussions that are interesting and important.

Several statistics related to the group is provided by LinkedIn. You can view statistics related to the demographics, member growth and activity of the group.

Make use of the publishing platform

Another best way to reach your target prospects is by making use of LinkedIn's publishing platform. The posts you make on the publishing platform are tied to your profile permanently. When a prospect visits your profile, your posts will also be displayed to him/her.

Here are a few important tips you need to follow to make an efficient use of the platform:

- See that the content you post is informative and is relevance to your target audience.

- You can use other social networking sites like twitter and Facebook to share your posts.

- Review the comments posted by audience and don't forget to respond to as many as you can.

- Use LinkedIn metrics for evaluating the performance of the content you post.

- Adding media like videos will help in drawing more visitors.

You can draw new customers to your business and develop an efficient marketing strategy in LinkedIn by following the steps discussed above.

Also, once you decide on a LinkedIn strategy, it is important that you show commitment towards it by being consistent and sincere.

Jonathan Martin

Chapter 7

Marketing Strategies for Instagram

Instagram is a popular social networking site that allows the sharing of photos and videos that have been captured through mobile phones. An average of 70 million photographs are generated on Instagram every day. Nearly 300 million users from around the world visit Instagram per month. The photo and video-sharing site is only 5 years old as of 2015, but has succeeded in attracting a large number of users, establishing its name in the list of top social networking sites.

Instagram is a very visual social media site that provides brands with a platform to build their identity and community base. It provides the brands with an opportunity to tell a compelling story about themselves using photographs and videos. Success on Instagram depends on factors like visual creativity, a well-thought out strategy and an ability to manage communities effectively.

For developing an effective marketing strategy for Instagram, you need to have clear objectives in the first place. Secondly, your results should be measurable. Here is a comprehensive guide that teaches you how to develop an effective marketing strategy for Instagram:

Clear Objectives

Irrespective of whether you are new to Instagram or an existing user who wants to boost your online presence, you need to ask yourself the following questions:

1. What sets apart Instagram from the other platforms?
2. Do you have a clear idea of who your target audience is?
3. How can Instagram be integrated with other social networking sites?

Instagram provides you with a visual platform that not only allows you to showcase your products and services, but also your people and culture. Instagram imparts a casual approach to the interaction that occurs between the brand and its followers, as it is a mobile-based app that lets you capture moments quickly and post them online instantaneously. Depending on the type of business you run and the performance indicators of your brand, the objectives of your Instagram strategy may be as follows:

- Promoting awareness about your brand
- Let people get an idea of your company culture
- Let people take a peek into your team
- Recruiting new talent
- Building customer engagement
- Building a loyal customer base
- Showcasing or demonstrating the workings of your products or services
- Enhancing event experiences.
- Building a strong community base
- Providing incentives to promote customer engagement
- Sharing news about your company
- Communicating with influencers
- Using a third party app for driving your sales

These objects will aid you in determining the best approaches to develop your strategy.

Create a strategy for your content

Content is the first and foremost factor that determines the success of your Instagram presence. Many businesses make use of Instagram to popularize their product. They mostly focus on recruiting new talent and showcasing their company culture. You need to create eye-catching content to attract the attention of your target audience as well as for the retention of existing customers. There is a risk of losing customers if the content is not regularly updated. Thus, retaining customers is as important too.

Content themes

Firstly, you need to decide what aspects of your brand you want to highlight in your content. This is can be decided based on what your objectives are. The subject of your content could be the working of your product, your services, and company culture or team members. Once you compile a list of themes you want to use for your content, you can choose a subject as the hero of your content. You can rotate between the subjects.

Some businesses focus on demonstrating and exhibiting their products or services, while the others choose a more creative way to showcase their product. For instance, Oreo goes the whimsical way by showcasing their cookies as a part of artworks. They creatively use their cookies to recreate landscapes or historical monuments.

Content types

Even though Instagram is primarily a photo-sharing app, it's content is not limited to photographs. Its users post creative content that range from simple images to animated GIFs or graphics. Before posting content to your Instagram account, you need to decide on what type of content best suits your business. You don't have to limit yourself to using a single type of content; you can use multiple types of contents, but see that you maintain a balance among them so as to optimally utilize your resources. Also, choose the content type that is mostly likely to promote engagement among your audience.

If a video could present your product in a compelling way, use videos more often in your content. If posting more videos is not feasible with your time or resources, you may not to post videos at all in your daily content and reserve them for promotions or campaigns. Quality of the content plays a major role in attracting the audience, so, it is advised that you spend more time on creating quality content, rather than posting mediocre content, the creation of which doesn't require much time or effort.

Content calendar

In order to elevate your presence on Instagram, you need to decide on how frequently you are going to post content to your account.

To decide on the frequency, it is advised that you create and maintain a content calendar that rotates your themes based on your campaigns and dates. Instagram doesn't have any feature that let's you schedule your posts. It also doesn't allow third party apps or tools to work with the publishing, which means you can neither create a schedule for your content on Instagram directly, nor can you use other social media apps or tools to create a schedule for you. So, you need to create your content beforehand and then prepare a content calendar for your team to follow. Thus, preparing your photos, videos or GIFs in advance is important for creating a schedule that decides when the content should go live.

Setting up a schedule for your content doesn't mean you have to rigidly follow whatever you have put on paper. Some of the best content on Instagram comes spontaneously from the events taking place on your company. You should create a schedule that is flexible enough to accommodate unplanned events. Be quick to publish such content so as to provide the audience with a glimpse of real-time social engagements.

User-Generated Content (UGC)

If your user community create content that features your brand and shares it own their own, it means you have hit the jackpot, as you will have access to a treasure of user-generated content.

You can curate the content created by your fans to engage your audience and encourage them to follow their own creative approaches in sharing content that depicts them interacting with your product or service. In Instagram's terms, sharing a user's content is called as 'regramming' the content. But how can you find such user-generated content that features your brand? User-generated content that features your product or service can be found by monitoring the hashtags of your brand. Be careful while choosing such user-generated content, as the content you choose should be in line with your brand aesthetic. Also, never share the content of a user without reviewing his/her account and also the other posts in the profile. When you share their photo, you are publicly aligning your brand with them, so make sure if it is safe and appropriate to do so.

Also, before sharing the user's content, it is a good practice to ask the user's permission. You can give credit to the original creator by using the @ symbol in your caption. That way, you encourage users to post more and more content that features your brand.

For instance, the popular furniture store Pottery Barn promotes its brand awareness by following an excellent strategy. It encourages users to mention the hashtag #mypotterybarn, if they want the brand to share their photos. When Pottery Barn regrams a user's photo, it mentions the user in the caption and compliments the original photographer. Most importantly, it also refers to the brand's item featured in the photograph.

Set clear-cut guidelines

If you want to build your brand on a social media site, your voice should be consistently heard on the platform. But, if you have multiple social media accounts for your business, it is difficult for you to manage and post content on all the sites all by yourself. So, what you would usually do is delegate the responsibility of handling multiple social media accounts to different people. Since different people may have different ideas or different levels of creativity, your brand's content may vary from one social media site to other. But, it is important that your content maintains a common tone on all of your social media accounts. So, it is necessary that you set some common guidelines for your team that manages the social media accounts of your brand. In case of Instagram, you need to let the person responsible for managing the account know certain guidelines regarding the composition of photographs and videos. Also, you need to set guidelines about the usage of filters and captions. Setting such guidelines will ensure that your brand's content on

Instagram maintains the same tone as that of the content on other sites. `

Creating a style guide

You need to set up a style guide that outlines the way you approach several features of Instagram, ranging from deciding what filter to use and tagging the locations. When you plan your approaches towards Instagram's features beforehand, you are maximizing them to their full potential.

Here are the features to which you need to define your approaches beforehand:

1. Composition: Social media marketers may possess some knowledge about photography, but not all of them are natural photographers. Even if the marketer is good at photography, the square frame used in Instagram is a step away from the portraits and landscape frames used in traditional photography.

You need to decide on the approach you are going to employ while dealing the following

.Subject
·White balance

·Color combination

·Background

You need to focus on these elements for creating visual harmony in the photographs.

2. Aesthetics of the brand: You need to take a look at how you visually represent your brand in general. Do you use established colors in representing your logos, ads, or websites? What tone do your brand's visuals usually have? Do they have a warm tone or a cool tone? The editing effects you use on Instagram should reflect the color palette of your brand's visual representations.

One of the examples of brands that have a well-established aesthetic and a well-defined composition is MailChimp. If you take a look at the how the brand is represented visually in general, you can notice that a single color dominates the background, making the subject standout.

3. Filters: You can edit your photographs or videos in several ways when using Instagram. While using the filters, see that their effects are consistent with the aesthetics of your brand. There are several filters available on Instagram, from which you need to choose only the ones that fit the color tone of your brand.

Another way of editing a photo on Instagram is to use the option Lux. Using this option (symbol which look like the sun), the saturation and contrast of the photograph can be adjusted. You can also use creative tools, which lets the user set the tone of the photograph by adjusting the brightness, warmth, color, shadows, contrast etc. When it comes to editing videos, you can apply filters to them, trim their length and set a specific image to be the cover image of the video.

4.Captions: In Instagram, the character limit for writing captions is 2,200. Different people approach captions differently. Some people never include captions in their content, while the others make use of captions to write short stories related to the photographs or videos they post. Although it seems like lengthy captions will deter users from following your posts, but no correlation has been found statistically between the size of the caption and user engagement. You need to set guidelines for using captions too, mainly in terms of the usage of emoticons, hashtags, sentence fragments and using the @ symbol to mention other users.

5.Hashtags: Discovering content on Instagram is made easy by using hashtags. Also, using hashtags helps users in finding accounts that they can follow. So, using them attracts new followers to your account and helps in elevating audience engagement. You can use up to a 30 hashtags in a comment or a post, so, you need to determine beforehand how many hashtags you are going to use in a typical post, or if you are going to use them at all. In a recent study conducted by Track Maven, it was shown that for accounts on Instagram whose followers are less than 1000 in number, using 11 hashtags per post attracted most engagement from the followers. On the other hand, it was shown that for accounts whose followers are more than 1000 in number, using 5 hashtags per post attracted most engagement form the followers. Also, you need to decide on if the hashtag created for your brand aligns with the theme chosen for your content.

6. Photo Map: You can use the 'add to photo map feature' for location-tagging of your photos. The advantage of location-tagging your posts is that, they attract higher audience engagement when compared to posts that are not location-tagged. It was found in a study that location-tagged posts receive 79% more interaction than normal posts. Location-tagging, which is also known as geo-tagging, is particularly useful for business that involves travelling to multiple destinations. For example, travel or tourism businesses can make effective use of this feature.

7. Tagging people: Instagram allows you to tag another Instagram user or brand in your past. When you do so, the other individual or brand will be notified of the post and they will be able to view it.

8. Sharing: Using Instagram, you can get connected to your profiles on other social media sites like Twitter, Facebook, Tumblr, Foursquare, Flickr etc, and can also share your Instagram photos on those sites. You need to decide if you should make use of this feature for cross-posting and promoting your Instagram posts.

Roles of your team members

If you have a social media marketing team, see that the social media manager is directly involved in marketing your brand on Instagram. It doesn't mean he has to take the sole responsibility of managing the account; other members of the team may also be encouraged to contribute to the Instagram content. Or you can divide the responsibility of the Instagram account among different members of the team in terms of content creation, managing the community, discovering people and publishing posts at the right time.

Jonathan Martin

Creating an effective Bio

You Instagram bio can contain up to 150 characters, so you need to include in the bio only what's important and worthy of mentioning of your brand. You can include your brand hashtags in your bio, but unlike a caption, a bio doesn't allow a user to click on those hashtags (in the mobile app). But the advantage of using your brand's hashtag in the bio is that users will come to know of its existence and use it to search for related posts.

Live links

The only place on Instagram wherein you can post live links is your bio. The only people who can make use of the space outside of it for live linking are advertisers. If you want to redirect people from your Instagram account to your website, the only way for you to do so is by including your website link in your profile.

Analyzing the performance

You need to analyze the performance of the content you post on Instagram by measuring its engagement. You can calculate engagement rate of a post by adding the likes and comments on a post and the dividing it with the number of users following the account at the time of making the post. You can use other metrics like the number of followers of your account, number of hashtag mentions and number of location tags to measure the success of your Instagram marketing strategy.

Thus, when used to its full potential, Instagram can help in skyrocketing the popularity of your business or brand.

Jonathan Martin

Chapter 8
Marketing Strategies for Snapchat

Most people disregard the lesser-known social media sites such as Snapchat because they aren't aware of the benefits that these sites have to promote one's work. So in this chapter we will look into how dominate on this social media site.

If you have never used Snapchat or don't exactly know what it does, it is a mobile based app whose functionality involves a user editing and sending a photo message to another user, which will get automatically deleted after the other user views it. Snapchat started out as a photo-messaging app meant for teenagers, but that's not the case anymore.

Snapchat is definitely fun to use and allows people to snap pictures or record videos that get deleted after playing for a few seconds. The user can decide on the number of seconds the photo or video has to play on the recipient's mobile. The sender can choose between 1 and 10 seconds before sending the image or video.

Here are a few statistics that demonstrate how popular Snapchat is as of 2015:

- Snapchat users share as many as 4 billion photographs and videos every day.

- As many as 100 million users login to their Snapchat accounts daily. It is no wonder that Snapchat is gradually becoming a favorite marketing tool for social media marketers

- Nearly 71 percent of Snapchat users (U.S) are of the ages between 18 and 34. Because of the rate at which it is growing, Snapchat can be employed as an important part of your marketing strategy. It provides you with a platform to build brand awareness and attract customers in a clever manner.

- Its users view Snapchat stories 500 million times every day.

- Facebook proposed to buy Snapchat for 3 billion dollars, but Snapchat rejected the proposal.

- The company is anywhere between 10-20 billion dollars worth.

The message format of Snapchat is short and sweet and can be employed by businesses, both big and small to generate daily stories that their customers could relate to.

The app also offers several photo editing tools like filters and also text message based features like emoticons, music etc.

Native content

When you use a social networking site for marketing your brand, you need to stick to the native content of the platform (i.e. content specific to it), to get better results. When it comes to Snapchat, the following are the types of content that are best suited to the platform:

- Humor

- Selfies

- Fleeting moments

- Controversies

- Embarrassing moments

- Simple and meaningless chats

- Silly chatter

You might wonder why any serious business or brand would choose a social media site that is mostly used for sharing silly, embarrassing and meaningless content?

If you want an answer to the question, all you need to know about is two things that make Snapchat not only unique from its social media counterparts, but also extremely useful for marketing a brand:

1. **The content disappears within seconds:**

If you fail to view the photo or video immediately after it is sent to you, it disappears. So, people keep coming back for more for the fear of missing out on funny or entertaining content.

2. People love to share and read stories:

People in general, especially those on the younger side love to share their personal experiences through beautifully woven stories. They also love watching similar stories of other people, whom they can relate to. If you are new to Snapchat, you need to get familiar with some widely used Snapchat terms:

- **Snaps**

These are the photographs or videos that have been captured in real-time and shared with other people instantly. Depending upon the length of time chosen by the sender, a recipient can view the snaps for up to ten seconds

• **Stories**

Stories are nothing but snaps that have been strung together to craft an interesting narrative. These stories last for 24 hours and can be created by adding Snaps to the narrative. Privacy can be set such that the stories can be viewed only by the Snapchatter's friends, or a particular group or all Snapchatters. These stories follow the conventions of true storytelling like the Snaps playing in a sequential order and having a proper beginning and ending.

Let's discuss how you can use Snapchat to promote your business or product. First, let's see what makes Snapchat so different from the other Social media sites. The brain behind Snapchat sure went to great lengths to make it stand it and it paid off! The developers came up with a social media platform that has only time-constrained image and video sharing facility. With at the maximum of 10 seconds of viewing, this app is popular with controversial pictures but it can also be used for marketing strategies. With the majority of the users being between 18 and 30, Snapchat is the most popular social media platform if you want to reach out to the youngsters. The tips given below will illustrate the ways to use Snapchat to your advantage.

#Think quick

Consider the fact that Snaps exist for just 10 seconds at the maximum. Ten seconds is all you have to captivate the Snapchatter so you need to use your snap wisely. The unique feature of this app is the one that makes it trickier for users. The self destruct option makes it all the more difficult for audiences to come back to a Snap so the Snap you send should be catchy yet have all the information the viewer needs.

#Draw

If there is any social media platform wherein you can go nuts with your creativity, it has to be Snapchat. It has a 'draw' feature, which can be used for transforming your snaps into something funny, though provoking or simply colorful. There is no limit for your imagination on Snapchat, and also your work won't get judged or criticized for what it is.

#Offer rewards and coupons

Snapchat's most popular trade is their discount offers and coupon messages. Because the quirkiness of Snapchat is its time limit, even these come with a limited time tag. The self-destruct also gives you an excuse for the expiration of the offer. So when your target audience knows that you have amazing offers but only a limited time they will have an extra incentive to keep checking your Snapchat. You could have contests where the prize could be a free sample of the new product or a behind the scenes tour. For example, a frozen yoghurt brand put up an offer where they encouraged Snapchatters to snap pictures of themselves eating yoghurt and receive discount coupons, if they managed to show it to the cashier within the 10 seconds it took to self-destruct.Or let's say you own a makeup line, you could offer a promo code to your customers that would give them a 5 percent discount for every photograph they submit of them using your mascara. Or you could hold a contest that requires the customers to post stories or pictures everyday showcasing how they're daily using the products of your makeup line for a week or so. You could pick a winner and send them a gift card that they can use to buy your products. These types of promotions that involve a business directly rewarding its customers help in establishing two-way communication and will result in an increase in user-generated content, which is loved by many customers.

Jonathan Martin

#Sneak peeks

Another way to keep your fans hooked is to give them sneak peeks of the new arrivals or collections. Sneak peeks are a great way to ensure that the product has an amazing first week of sales and what better place to give a sneak peek than a place where the image gets destroyed after 10 seconds.

#Sales and events

Snapchat is a good way to keep your customers informed of any event or sales that are happening or going to happen. Flash sales are a tactic that you can use to attract a large number of customers for a short period of time. One of the major advantages of using Snapchat is its ability to facilitate users with real time-access to trade shows or other live events. Even if you don't hold a trade show for your product, you can still employ Snapchat creatively for your business so as to attract the attention of prospective customers. For example, if you own a pet store that sells pet accessories and food, you can use Snapchat to announce drum-sales as follows: Be one of the first ten customers to buy three packets of dog food and receive a fluffy pet toy for FREE! Or if you have a fast food joint, you could announce something like this: Be one of the first five customers to grab our macaroni pizza and relish a delicious brownie for FREE! Such direct and unexpected announcements will create excitement and buzz among the audience, and will fetch you customers

#Exclusive promos

By releasing footage of exclusive behind the scenes videos and images of products or clothes you are giving the fans something to look forward. If that exclusive promo captivates the audience then the chances of them liking the product are much higher. A technique that can be used is the "guess what the image is" promotion. While that might be difficult to control on Snapchat, it has been used with a lot of success on Facebook and Twitter. It is important that you remember every social media account you have should be used to post content that is exclusive to the users of the site. There is no real harm in sharing the same content across various platforms, but make sure that there at least some content that is unique to Snapchat. For example, if you have launched a makeup product, you can share on Snapchat your personal story and inspiration behind the product. You should try to make Snapchatters feel that are seeing something special which the users of other social media sites cannot see.

Being genuine rules

There is no place for fakeness or phoniness on Snapchat. Snapchat users don't come to Snapchat to see formal or boring details about your product. They have your official company website for that. Also, Snapchat doesn't allow you to share images that you have downloaded or captured elsewhere. You can share an image on Snapchat only if you have clicked it using the app. This means, only, genuine and authentic photographs that have been captured in the moment can be shared on Snapchat. So, never try to capture a moment that has been staged as the fakeness will show in the image. Also, try not to sound too corporate or formal. Snapchat is not a place for such corporate talk.

#Let young people manage the account

The first thing you need to remember when on Snapchat is that, people won't expect you to sound like a logo, they expect you to sound like a person. You should come across to them as an approachable, friendly and easy-going person with whom they can share cool stuff. As we have already seen, every social networking site aims at a particular user demographic. When it comes to Snapchat, its audience base mainly consists of the younger folk and millennials. If you have young interns or assistants or young people working for you, give them the task of managing the account, for they will know how the younger generation rolls.

#Be consistent

The common pattern usually observed in businesses joining social media sites is that, they enter the platform with a big boom, but gradually become inconsistent in posting content and interacting with customers. When it comes to Snapchat, content is really the king. People won't care if you have an account; all they will ever care about is your content, that too only if it's creative and interesting. So, make your presence felt at least twice or thrice a week by posting snaps. Make sure that you're consistent in posting content regularly and increase the frequency during the times of product launches or special events.

#Introduce a new product

Introduce your new product first on Snapchat the day before it is released in your stores or on any online stores. You could even create a Story so that you update a new feature of the product on each day of the week prior to the release of the product. That way the customers are already enthusiastic about the product before it is even launched. However, keep some element of surprise for the end. Let that be an incentive for your viewers to try the product or come see it themselves on the day of release. Urban Decay, a makeup brand made use of the Snapchat platform for creating anticipation among the users before launching their new eye shadow. They had a total of 5,60,000 followers on Twitter, to whom they had announced that they are active ion Snapchat too. Many of the followers who also had a Snapchat account added them to their account and waited in anticipation for the launch of the new product.

#Be creative

This is something every Snapchatter should be if they want to draw attention to themselves. If you plan to market your brand make sure that besides the actual marketing strategies you have fun things to Snap about even when you have no new product lined up for the customers. If you just a regular user looking for more followers, be creative with what you share on Snapchat. Try not to share just pictures of your face or what you are doing. People are more likely to be interested in weird things that they don't see very often. For example, a weird cloud shape or water droplet or beautiful scenery are some of the things that would make people interested. Find things to record that will attract a lot of people even if it is something as mundane as a pretty flower. Diversity in Snaps is a good way to keep people on their toes hoping for what they might see next time.

#Behind the scenes

As with Snapchat and other social media platforms giving your followers a sneak peek or a behind the scenes glance can go a long way in garnering more followers. As we have already seen, Snapchat is an app for capturing and sharing moments real-time. You can let your audience take a peek at your company culture, working environment, teasers, or even happy photographs of your employees. Do you own a bakery? Then post an image of your chef working on a funny looking cake (like SpongeBob Square Pants). Or if you want to promote a clothing brand then post shots of the makeup room or the rehearsals to the big reveal or fashion show. Such things will keep the audience interested.

#Put yourself into your posts

Instead of making your posts seem like run of the mill kind of posts, add a bit of yourself into it. Once your followers know that you are taking the effort to get involved they will automatically warm up to you more. A funny caption or a witty statement is all your post needs for it to catch the eye of the users. Humor also helps create a strong bond between you and your followers.

Partner with star users

The main disadvantage of using Snapchat to promote your brand is that, attracting large number of followers is more difficult when compared to other social networking sites. But the issue can be dealt with if you could approach the star users (influencers) of Snapchat. Just like every other social networking site, Snapchat has very popular users who could lead a large number of users to your account. You can amass a great number of followers if you could identify approach and partner with such star users. These influencers will play their part in marketing your product; they could create a crafty video of them enjoying a cheeseburger at your food joint or might post pictures of them donning the new line of mascara launched by you. Whatever may be the product, a star user does have the power to influence users into following you and buying your products.

#*Show your fun side*

Do you and team members go out on company outings? Do you celebrate birthdays at the office? Or is your company involved in a cause? Capturing and sharing the photographs or videos of such events, causes or outings will unmask the fun and human-side of your business to your customers. If you and your team went out on a hiking trip, post the images of your team members in action and having fun. However dispassionate the customer may be, such content will make them feel that they are a member of the tribe. This is one way of letting your customers know that you are more than just a brand and have a human side too.

Snapchat is different when it comes to measuring success

Snapchat is not like other platforms when it comes to measuring popularity and success. On twitter, you could keep track of the retweets, and on Facebook, you could keep track of the shares of your post. There are no such features on Snapchat. You can't measure your success on Snapchat using the same metrics that are used by other social networking sites. But there is one way you can measure the popularity your snap on Snapchat. Whenever a user takes captures a snap by taking a screenshot of it, the sender gets notified of the screenshot. By keeping track of the number of screenshots earned by your snap, you can measure its popularity.

Even though Snapchat is a relatively young social media site, it possesses a lot of potential when it comes marketing a product or a brand. All you need to have is a bit of quirkiness and creativity. Also, we are in an age where we have lots of distractions and a very short attention span. Snapchat is the only social media site right now that takes advantage of this issue. Even though this site is not as popular as Facebook or twitter, it won't be long before it takes the reins of social networking and stands beside the likes of Facebook.

.

Conclusion

To conclude, social media presents still growing and exciting opportunities for creative and meaningful marketing conversations. The landscape is ever evolving to explore even more sophisticated ways of connecting with the global population. We are still working to provide continued and sustained Internet to the majority of the world's population, which still do not have access to electricity, let alone the Internet. These efforts, though daunting have had a lot of successes - opening up the medium to a huge population and thus broadening its potential.

Most social web networks are exploring the potential of Augmented Reality to expand social networking in a physical sense. The concepts of Augmented Reality are still in a nascent stage despite the groundbreaking future that is envisioned by the concept. The potential of Augmented Reality in web marketing derives from the increased interactions and communications that social networking as it stands today has only hinted at.

Marketing and advertising was slow on the uptake with social networking, but in the short time that the market has embraced social media the market has exploded - more and more brands are trying to tap into the market in different ways. Social media has granted brands the unique opportunity to present to potential customers a human side to the brands, which the sphere of advertising had hitherto not been able to enter. Advertisements have traditionally been associated with the Internet, with several website making all their money from them. However it has only been with the recognition of the potential of social networking that they have taken to the Internet in such a manner. The advent of mobile internet and the corresponding rise in the number of people connected to the internet, and the potential of Augmented Reality with the chance of being connected with the global populace in real time and in a physical sense means that marketing needs to evolve and grow along with the audiences and always be on the lookout for newer and more interesting ways to connect with audiences. The human touch that social networking has provided to marketing has proved to be a fresh breath of air for a service which many feared would no longer be relevant. It has been said that a brand on a social network ascends through three cycles:

the first when the audience likes the content and the brand, the second when the audience 'loves' the brand, and the exclusive third cycle which every brand should aspire to become: one that is defended by their audience. That is, elicit such an emotional response in the audience that they would defend the brand, both in social media, and in day-to-day interactions. This is the trajectory of a successful social media strategy.

I hope you enjoyed perusing this book, and hope that it provides some new directions for your company or brand to take with respect to social networking.

Free Bonus

Here is a free guide to help you grow your social media following enjoy!

https://publishfs.leadpages.co/social-media-brand-go-2/

www.ingramcontent.com/pod-product-compliance
Lightning Source LLC
Chambersburg PA
CBHW051328170526
45166CB00002B/723